Tiger Talk
People I Know

Mom and Dad

Leon Read

SEA-TO-SEA
Mankato Collingwood London

Contents

Different families   **4**

Having fun   **6**

Animal families   **8**

Teaching us   **10**

Things I like...   **12**

Feeling better   **14**

Going to work   **16**

Real names   **18**

Playing house   **20**

Me and my family   **22**

Word picture bank   **24**

Look for Tiger on the pages of this book. Sometimes he is hiding.

Moms and dads are part of a family.

Every family is different.

Different families

Moms and dads are different, too!

My dad is good at drawing.

Our dad is cool!

My mommy has black hair.

My mom loves cuddles.

Jacob used a camera to take pictures of his mom and dad.

Having fun

Belonging to a family is fun.

Kira's dad gives her
a piggyback ride.

I am flying!

6

7

Animal families

Sharon and Tiger are playing
with a family of chimpanzees.

Now the chimps
are hiding from
Tiger!

Lions

Elephants

Geese

What other animal
families can you
think of?

Teaching us

Moms and dads teach us many things.

From the alphabet,

to counting.

From how
to behave,

to how to
play games.

My dad taught
me to play
Crazy Eights.

Things I like...

There are special things we like to do with our mom and dad.

I like reading with my daddy.

I like going to the playground with Mommy.

I like playing soccer with my dad.

What special things do you like to do?

Feeling better

Moms and dads
help us to feel better.

Dad cheers up Carmel.

Harry's
mom makes
him laugh.

Peter's dad gives him a bandage.

Emma is sick. Her mom looks after her.

When was the last time you felt sick or upset?

15

Going to work

Many moms and dads go out
to work to earn money.

Some people work inside.

Some people work outside.

What job do you want to do when you grow up?

Real names

Moms and dads have real names, just like us.

My daddy's name is Michael.

Riaz

Jane

Sarah

Sam

Most people have a middle name, too.

My middle name is Clive.

What is your middle name?

19

Playing house

Michelle likes playing pretend families with Freddie.

Mom is looking after the baby.

It is fun playing families.

Daddy is cooking dinner.

Me and my family

Sharon is drawing a picture of her family.

I am drawing my mommy first.

Draw a picture of your family.

Who are the important people in your life?

Word picture bank

Cuddles—P. 5

Sick—P. 15

Letters—P. 10

Piggyback—P. 6

Playground—P. 13

Crazy Eights—P. 11

This edition first published in 2010 by Sea-to-Sea Publications
Distributed by Black Rabbit Books
P.O. Box 3263, Mankato, Minnesota 56002
Copyright © Sea-to-Sea Publications 2010

Printed in USA

9 8 7 6 5 4 3 2

Published by arrangement with the Watts Publishing Group Ltd,
London.

Library of Congress Cataloging-in-Publication Data
Read, Leon.
  Mom and dad / Leon Read.
    p. cm. -- (Tiger talk. People I know)
  Includes index.
  ISBN 978-1-59771-192-0 (hardcover)
  1. Parents--Juvenile literature. 2. Family--Juvenile literature. I. Title.
HQ755.8.R383 2010
306.874--dc22

                                    2008048581

Series editor: Adrian Cole
Photographer: Andy Crawford (unless otherwise credited)
Design: Sphere Design Associates
Art director: Jonathan Hair
Consultants: Prue Goodwin and Karina Law
Acknowledgments:
The Publisher would like to thank Norrie Carr model agency. "Tiger" puppet used
with kind permission from Ravensden PLC (www.ravensden.co.uk). Tiger Talk logo
drawn by Kevin Hopgood. Photo credits: cover Patricia Marks/Shutterstock. 1, 3bl, 6r,
19b, 24bl Edyta Pawlowska/ Shutterstock. 3t HTuller/Shutterstock. 3br Olga Lyubkina/
Shutterstock. 4t Yuri Arcurs/Shutterstock. 4b, 11b, 24br Karen Struthers/ Shutterstock.
5t, 12 digitalskillet/Shutterstock. 5c, 24tl Anna Chelnokova/Shutterstock. 5b, 6l
Losevsky Pavel/Shutterstock. 7t, 19t Glenda M. Powers/Shutterstock. 7b iofoto/
Shutterstock. 9l Kristian Sekulic/Shutterstock. 9c Norma Cornes/Shutterstock. 9r Jeff
Thrower (WebThrower)/ Shutterstock. 10t, 24tr Elena Schweitzer/Shutterstock. 10b
Matka Wariatka/Shutterstock. p 11t Tomasz Trojanowski/Shutterstock.
13t, 24bc Fei Dongliang/Shutterstock. 13b Elena Elisseeva/
Shutterstock. 14t 2734725246/ Shutterstock.
14b Jaimie Duplass/Shutterstock.
15t Bettina Baumgartner/Shutterstock.
15b, 24tc Jamie Wilson/Shutterstock.
16 Radu Razvan/Shutterstock.
17t+b Stephen Coburn/Shutterstock.
18 Jason Stitt/Shutterstock.

There are 18 Tigers, including me, in this book.
Did you find all of us?